THE WORLD'S MOST A...

CRIME FACTS

For Kids

First published in Great Britain in 2003 by
Egmont Books Limited,
239 Kensington High Street,
London W8 6SA

Copyright © 2003 Egmont Books Limited

ISBN 0 603 56097 0

1 3 5 7 9 10 8 6 4 2

Printed and bound in the U.A.E.

THE WORLD'S MOST AMAZING

CRIME FACTS

For Kids

Written and Compiled by Guy Campbell & Mark Devins
Illustrated by Paul Moran

CONTENTS

LOOPY LAWS

Some Very Strange Laws

In New Mexico, USA, women are strictly forbidden to appear unshaven in public.

According to a British law passed in 1845, attempting to commit suicide was a crime punishable by the death penalty.

An old Boston law requires that you must get a prescription to take a bath.

A New York state law declared that any person riding in a lift cannot talk to anyone, and must keep his or her eyes looking forwards at the elevator door at all times with their hands in a folded position until they leave.

In England in 1571, a man could be fined for not wearing a wool cap.

In Florida, USA, women can be fined for falling asleep under a hair dryer, as can the salon owner for letting them.

In Fairbanks, Alaska, it is illegal for a moose to be on the pavement. This dates back to the early days of the town when the owner of a bar had a pet moose that he used to get drunk. The moose would then stumble around the town inebriated. The only way the authorities could prevent this from happening was to create the law stopping the moose from crossing the pavement to get access to the bar.

In Sparta during the 4th century BC, if you were male and over 20 years of age, you were required by law to eat two pounds of meat a day. It was supposed to make you brave.

It is against the law to whale hunt in Oklahoma, a landlocked American state.

In the 16th century, King François I of France made the wearing of whiskers punishable by death.

Massachusetts in the US has a law that prohibits using bullets as a form of currency.

Also in Massachusetts, state laws decree that mourners at a gathering after a funeral may not eat more than three sandwiches, and that snoring is prohibited unless all your bedroom windows are closed and securely locked. Plus ... an old law declares goatee beards to be illegal unless you first pay a special licence fee for the privilege of wearing one.

Posting a building has been illegal in the US since 1916 when a man mailed a 40,000-ton brick house across Utah to avoid freight rates.

In Nebraska, USA, a parent can be arrested if his child cannot hold back a burp during a church service.

Hypnotism is banned in public schools in San Diego, USA.

In the US town of Grants Pass, Oregon, you can throw onions at "obnoxious salesmen" if they won't stop knocking on your door.

By law, in Bourbon, Missouri, USA, one small onion must be served with each glass of water in a restaurant.

In Tamarack, Idaho, in the US, you can't buy onions after dark without a special permit from the sheriff.

In Somalia, Africa, it is illegal to carry old chewing gum stuck on the tip of your nose.

In the American state of Utah, birds have the right of way on all highways.

The sale of chewing gum is outlawed in Singapore because it is a means of "tainting an environment free of dirt".

In Finland, people must be able to read in order to get married.

In Greece, if you are unbathed or poorly dressed while driving on the public roads of Athens, you may have your driving licence taken away.

It is against the law for a woman weighing over 200 pounds and wearing shorts to be seen eating onions in a restaurant or at a public picnic in Ridgeland, South Carolina, USA.

By law, no shop is allowed to sell a toothbrush on the Sabbath in Providence, Rhode Island, USA. Yet these same shops are allowed to sell toothpaste and mouthwash on that day.

According to a 1649 Massachusetts law, punishment for stubbornness in children over the age of 16 was death.

In 1837 a British judge ruled that if a man kissed a woman against her will she was legally allowed to bite his nose off.

In Hartford, Connecticut, USA, you may not, under any circumstances, cross the street walking on your hands.

In Sarasota, Florida, USA, it's illegal to sing in a public place while attired in a swimsuit, and men may not be seen publicly in any kind of strapless gown.

In Chester, England, you can only shoot a Welsh person with a bow and arrow inside the city walls and after midnight.

In Switzerland, it is illegal to flush the toilet after 10 p.m. if you live in a flat.

In Gainesville, Georgia, USA, it is illegal to eat chicken with a fork.

A law in International Falls, Minnesota, USA, makes it illegal for cats to chase dogs up telephone poles in the city.

It is illegal to cross the state boundaries of Iowa with a duck on your head.

During the great plague in the 14th century, a law was passed that people should say "God bless you" to anyone who sneezed. At the time it was believed that the sneezes were a way of expelling evil from the body.

In Cleveland, Ohio, USA, it's illegal to catch mice without a hunting licence.

In Utah, USA, it is illegal to swear in front of a dead person.

In the 1940s, Californian law made it illegal to dress as a member of the opposite sex. Drag queens avoided the restriction by attaching pieces of paper to their dresses which read "I'm a boy". The courts accepted the argument that anyone wearing such a notice was technically dressed as a man, not a woman.

It is against the law to remove your shoes if your feet smell bad while you're in a theatre in Winnetka, Illinois, USA.

During the reign of Catherine I of Russia, men weren't allowed to get drunk before nine o'clock. And ladies weren't allowed to get drunk at all.

In Blue Hill, Nebraska, USA, no woman wearing a "hat which would scare a timid person" can be seen eating onions in public.

It was illegal for women to wear buttons in 15th-century Florence.

In Florida, a special law prohibits unmarried women from parachuting on Sundays. And if an elephant is left tied to a parking meter, the parking fee has to be paid just as it would for a vehicle.

In Milan, Italy, there is a law that requires a smile on the face of all citizens at all times. Exemptions include time spent visiting patients in hospitals or attending funerals. Otherwise, the fine is £60.

In Massachusetts, USA, it is illegal to go to bed without first having a full bath.

Women were banned by royal decree from using hotel swimming pools in Jiddah, Saudi Arabia, in 1979.

Texas is the only state in the US that permits residents to vote from space. The first to exercise this right to vote while in orbit was astronaut David Wolf, who cast his vote for Houston mayor via e-mail from the Russian space station Mir in November 1997.

A law in Harper Woods, Michigan, USA, makes it illegal to paint sparrows for the purpose of selling them as parakeets.

It was once against the law to slam your car door in cities in Switzerland.

In Kentucky, USA, anyone who has been drinking is legally "sober" until he or she "cannot hold onto the ground". Also, it is illegal to transport an ice-cream cone in your pocket.

Reportedly, in Saudi Arabia a woman may divorce her husband if he does not keep her supplied with coffee.

An old law in Jonesboro, Georgia, USA, made it illegal to use the expression "Oh, boy!" This came about because a man who lived in Jonesboro, who was elderly and wealthy, would often hire young boys to do work for him by calling out to them, "Oh, boy!" Some teenagers started to shout "Oh, boy!" every time they saw him. The man got fed up with this and, as he had quite a bit of influence in the community, he had the law passed that made it illegal to say "Oh, boy!" in public. However, the teenagers had the last laugh. When they saw him in public after that, one of them would yell, "Oh ..." and another would yell, "... boy!"

In the US town of Lexington, Kentucky, women cyclists cannot wear a swimsuit unless they're escorted by two policemen.

NOT A SHOPPING LIST

America's Most Wanted

America's Most Wanted Criminals list started in 1949, when a reporter wrote a story about the "toughest guys" sought by the Federal Bureau of Investigation. In response, the FBI provided ten names of wanted criminals.

The article created a sensation. Delighted at the subsequent publicity, FBI Director J. Edgar Hoover began the Ten Most Wanted Fugitives programme in March 1950. Since then the list has become a standard crime-fighting tool for the FBI. By widely circulating the lists to the media, the FBI has been able to enlist public help in finding what it calls "serious offenders".

Of the 458 names that have appeared on the list, 429 have been apprehended, including 137 as a direct result of tips from the public.

At first, bank robbers, burglars and car thieves dominated the list. In the 1960s, more fugitives were charged with destruction of property, sabotage and kidnapping. As organised crime and political terrorism increased in the 1970s, the make-up of the list changed again, and today, organised crime bosses, drug dealers, terrorists and serial killers dominate. To be on the list, a suspect must be especially dangerous, and authorities must believe that publicity would increase the chances of arrest.

Fugitives stay on the list until they are captured, or the charges against them are dropped, or they are no longer a menace to society, or they die.

YO HO HO!

Pirate Facts & Funnies

The word "pirate" simply means someone who robs or plunders on the sea. Today piracy is just a term for sea-robbery – any robbery committed under the laws of the Admiralty, rather than the laws of the land.

To stress the point that a pirate's crimes had been committed within the jurisdiction of the British Admiralty, 18th-century pirates were hanged at low-tide mark at Wapping in London. Below the low-tide mark counted as Admiralty territory; anything above it was for the civil courts to deal with.

As far back as the 6th century BC, pirates were robbing trading ships in ancient Greece.

The Roman Empire battled constantly against pirates stealing their grain imports.

In the 1500s, the Barbarossa (Redbeard) brothers, Aruj and Kheir-ed-din, roamed the Mediterranean. These "corsairs" were feared throughout the Mediterranean for their ferocious attacks on Christian ships and coastal settlements.

In the 16th century, British "privateers" such as Sir Francis Drake and Sir John Hawkins attacked Spanish galleons and relieved them of looted treasures from South America in the name of the British crown. "Letters of Marque" were issued to privateers by the British, permitting them to rob the Spanish whenever they could. The success of their voyages encouraged others, who didn't restrict their attacks to Spanish ships but took any vessel that might hold a valuable cargo. King James I withdrew all the Letters of Marque in 1603.

**Scotland has made its contribution
to the fact and fiction surrounding
the pirate:**

Scottish writers have played a major role in
the development of pirate mythology.
J.M. Barrie wrote the tale of *Peter Pan*,
taking many of the characteristics of
the evil Captain Hook from the notorious
real-life pirate, Blackbeard.
Robert Louis Stevenson wrote the
classic *Treasure Island*, which features
the most famous fictional pirate
of all: Long John Silver.
There have been real-life
Scottish pirates, too: in the 18th century,
a Scottish sixpence was recovered
from the wreck off the American
coast of pirate Black Sam Bellamy's
flagship, the *Whydah*, which indicated
that the pirate crew was
at least partly Scots.

The classic pirate era continued into the 18th century when many of the most notorious buccaneers roamed the seas. The two women pirates, Mary Read and Anne Bonny, were active between 1710 and 1720; Black Sam Bellamy roamed the coast of colonial America from early 1716 to mid 1717; and the infamous Blackbeard was killed in 1718 after two years of terrorising Caribbean seafarers.

Privateers made a comeback during the American Revolution (1775-83) when hundreds boosted the small American Navy and attacked English merchant ships, crippling trade. Scottish-born John Paul Jones' daring raids on behalf of the American Navy made him an American national hero.

For 30 years, from 1690 to 1720, the island of Madagascar was the principal base of the pirates preying on the rich trade of the Indian Ocean. Barely explored, Madagascar was the ideal hiding place for pirates driven out of the Caribbean. A visitor at the end of the 17th century counted 17 pirate vessels and an estimated population of 1,500 buccaneers.

By the beginning of the 19th century, navies no longer needed the help of the privateers. The introduction of steam-powered ships meant that pirates could be easily pursued and caught. It was the beginning of the end for the buccaneers.

Today, piracy has been largely wiped out along the main trade routes but in Southeast Asia and some parts of the Caribbean, piracy is still alive and well. The same cannot be said of some of their victims.

It was common for arguments to arise on long passages at sea. Strict rules were used to settle these disputes and ensure that booty was equally shared. Rules varied from ship to ship, but here is one pirate captain's example of a rulebook:

1. Every man shall obey command.
2. The captain shall have one full share and a half in all prizes.
3. The master, carpenter, boatswain and gunner shall have one share and a quarter.
4. Any man wishing to leave ship shall be marooned, with a bottle of powder, a bottle of water, one small arm, and shot.
5. Every man has a vote in all affairs.
6. No person to gamble aboard ship at cards or dice for money.
7. No striking on board, but every quarrel to be ended on shore, by sword and pistol.
8. No boy or woman is to be allowed among the crew.

The pirate flag was designed to strike fear into victims and encourage a hasty surrender. However, the black Jolly Roger commonly associated with pirates was not as greatly feared as the red flag, which meant that no mercy would be shown in battle. The Jolly Roger often depicted symbols of death and may have got its name from a nickname for the devil – Old Roger – but is more likely derived from the French name for the red flag – Jolie Rouge.

Pirates lived in times when navigation was primitive and printed maps were not widely available. To be successful, pirates had to position themselves across the known trade routes. After taking a prize, the pirates would flee to a bolthole, perhaps the island of Madagascar or some tiny Caribbean islet. Maps and navigational tools were vital and often the most valuable booty captured from the victim ships.

The cutlass evolved from the knives used by the original buccaneers to cut meat for barbecues. Its short blade made it ideal for use in confined spaces and it was the favoured weapon of nearly all pirates.

With its shortened barrel, the musketoon wasn't accurate, but it was easy to use on board where enemies were close and accuracy was not essential. It was the gun of choice for the discerning buccaneer.

The flintlock was light and the ideal weapon for boarding a victim ship. But if the powder got damp, the gun wouldn't fire, and it could fire only one shot at a time. So a pirate would carry several, and use them as clubs when all his bullets had gone.

A boarding axe was used to climb the sides of a ship. Once on deck, the axe could bring down sails to prevent escape.

When they reached a port, pirates liked to party, spending an absolute fortune on drink and gambling. But there is no rest for the wicked, and there was a lot of hard work to be done before they could sail again. The ship had to be serviced, which meant "careening" – the awful job of scraping all the barnacles off the hull. The sails and rigging had to be repaired and replaced, while other crew members would have the job of finding fresh water and food for the next voyage, which might be several months long. And, of course, there was treasure to bury!

Although the rewards of piracy could be great, the punishment for convicted pirates was to "dance the hempen jig", a pirate term for being hanged. The hanging was a public event which, in London, always took place at Execution Dock at Wapping.

Convicted pirates were taken from prison in a procession led by an officer carrying a silver oar – the symbol of the Admiralty – to the gallows at the low-tide mark. After a sermon from the chaplain, the pirate could address the crowd before execution. After execution, the bodies were left until three tides had washed over them, as a warning to others.

The preservation of food was a major problem for pirates, or indeed any seafarers of the time, before the invention of refrigeration and canned goods. Bottles of beer were preferred over water, which quickly became undrinkable. The staple food was "hard tack" – horrible hard biscuits. For very long voyages, limes would provide vitamin C to prevent scurvy, and hens on board the ship could provide both fresh eggs and meat. The main source of meat in the Caribbean were turtles, which could be picked up on any beach; they made for good eating.

The cat o' nine tails was a whip with many lashes, used for flogging lawbreakers on board a pirate ship. A "taste of the cat" might be a full flogging, or just a single blow to "smarten up" an unruly deckhand.

Keelhauling was the hideous punishment of dragging a man under the ship with ropes, from one side to the other. The victim of a keelhauling would be half-drowned, or worse, and lacerated by the barnacles that grew on the ship's hull. Walking the plank is the most famous piratical execution, beloved of makers of pirate-themed movies for a century. The victim, usually blindfolded and with bound hands, is forced to walk along a plank laid over the ship's side, until he falls into the water below. This punishment first appeared in 19th-century fiction, long after the great days of piracy, and is thought not to have been practised in reality.

YOUR MONEY OR YOUR LIFE

The Ways of Highwaymen

Highwaymen were common in England from the 14th century, when the country was pretty lawless. There were several peaks in their numbers however: just after the English Civil War (1642-1649) when soldiers from disbanded armies took to the road, and between 1697 and 1701, when the same happened with soldiers returning from the wars in France. The real golden age, however, was between 1700 and 1800, when it was rare not to be attacked on the road and many people actually wrote their wills before setting off on a coach trip.

Many highwaymen were of gentlemanly birth. There was little shame at the time in being recognised as a highwayman, and to be robbed by a famous one was regarded as something of an honour.

Victims were mostly the wealthy, and highwaymen were popular with the common folk, who didn't mind about the rich gentry getting held up. Highwaymen had a reputation for generosity with their loot, so they could usually be assured of a warm reception at the inns and pubs they visited.

By the end of the 18th century, the heyday of the English highwaymen was about over. Faster coaches, more traffic and better roads made holding up travellers trickier. Pub landlords were refused licences if they were known to harbour highwaymen, and the Government started posting horse patrols along the approach roads to London.

DICK TURPIN

Legend or Lightweight?

Dick Turpin's most famous and daring exploit was a ride from London to York on his faithful mare, Black Bess, in less than 24 hours. But it isn't true. This great ride was made by another highwayman, John "Swift Nick" Nevison, who made the ride of more than 190 miles in 15 hours to establish an alibi. It was attributed to Turpin in a novel and repeated in magazines, cheap novels and ballads.

Even today, there are so many inns along the Great North Road that boast Dick Turpin stopped there for a drink on his epic ride, he would have fallen off his horse long before he reached York!

Though Dick Turpin is often thought of today as the image of the dashing, gallant highwayman, he was little more than a burglar, a murderer and a horse thief.

Born in 1706 in rural Essex, Turpin served an apprenticeship with a butcher. When he had served it, he opened his own butcher's shop, and began to steal sheep, lamb and cattle as a sideline to fill his shelves. Caught in the act of stealing two oxen, he fled into the Essex countryside, where he tried his hand at smuggling. There he became a member of the notoriously vicious Essex Gang, an appalling bunch who started out as deer-rustlers before branching out into looting churches and robbing farmhouses. It was only after most of the gang were hanged, when one of their number gave them up to the police, that Turpin took to the road, at first in company with another highwayman,

"Captain" Tom King. King and Turpin worked in Waltham Forest, robbing passers-by. By 1737, Turpin had a £200 bounty on his head. The partnership came to an end when Turpin stole a horse that was tracked to the Red Lion pub in Whitechapel. When King came to collect the stolen animal, he was arrested. Turpin, waiting nearby, fired at the constables holding King, but he was a terrible shot and managed to shoot King instead. Turpin fled for Yorkshire, where he started horse-dealing under the name John Palmer.

He came to the attention of the local authorities when he shot his landlord's rooster, and threatened to do the same to the landlord. While he was held in custody, he was identified by his former schoolmaster as being none other than the notorious highwayman Dick Turpin himself. Convicted on two charges, Turpin was hanged at York on 19 April, 1739.

PLUNKET AND MACLAINE

The Prince and the Pauper

Plunket and MacLaine were the subjects of a movie in the 1990s, but they were not fictional creations.

James MacLaine lived by day as a gentleman in London's St James's, while his accomplice, William Plunket, lived nearby in rather more humble circumstances. MacLaine was born in 1742, the son of a minister in the north of Ireland. He took his father's inheritance to Dublin where, aged 18, he blew the lot on gambling and women. Shunned by his family, he moved to England, married an innkeeper's daughter and set up as a grocer. When his gambling ruined the business and his wife died, he struck up the famed criminal partnership with fellow bankrupt, Plunket. With stolen pistols and horses and their faces hidden by Venetian masks, they had a short but highly successful career as highwaymen. Despite rickety beginnings (MacLaine fled from their first robbery), the pair committed around 20 hold-ups in six months, often in Hyde Park, and claimed many famous victims.

During the hold-up of politician and writer Horace Walpole, MacLaine managed to shoot him accidentally, but the next day he wrote him a very polite letter apologising for any inconvenience caused.

The robberies were always conducted in a restrained and courteous fashion, earning MacLaine the "gentleman highwayman" tag and giving him enough money finally to live the society lifestyle he'd always craved. Actually most of the credit for their success should go to Plunket, as MacLaine was something of a coward who preferred to pursue women rather than wave a pistol about.

MacLaine was arrested when he tried to sell a very distinctive coat that he'd stolen from one Lord Elgington. The coat was recognised and MacLaine was caught.

Such was MacLaine's fame among the fashionable that his trial at the Old Bailey court was a social occasion, and in Newgate prison he reputedly received several thousand visitors, among them many high-society ladies attracted by his dangerous reputation. He was hanged in front of a crowd at Tyburn on 3 October, 1750.

Despite being blamed by his partner for every crime they had committed, Will Plunket was smart enough to escape with both his money ... and his life.

CLAUDE DUVAL

A Pleasure to be Robbed By

Claude Duval was French, born in 1643. He came to England with Royalists returning after the restoration of Charles II to the throne. By 1666 he had picked up a new trade: highway robbery.

His reputation as a dashing sort grew and was soon so widespread that some of his lady victims were actually delighted to be robbed by him. In 1670, Duval held up a coach containing a nobleman and his lady. To show she wasn't afraid, the lady took out a pipe and played a tune. Cheeky Duval asked her to dance, and afterwards relieved her husband of four hundred pounds. Taking a hundred, he gave the rest back to the lady in return for the dance. He became a romantic hero, though his capture was not quite as glorious. He was apprehended at a pub in London, and sent to Newgate prison, where he was tried by judge Sir William Morton. Despite efforts by the ladies of the court, and even the King himself, Sir William refused to change his death sentence. Duval was hanged on 21 January 1670.

He faced his end bravely, before an audience of screaming ladies – many of noble birth – wearing masks to disguise themselves.

Following a grand funeral at St Paul's Cathedral, Duval is said to have been buried beneath the aisle, with the following epitaph:

"Here lies Du Vall. Reader, if male thou art, Look to thy purse. If female, to thy heart. Much havoc has he made of both; for all men he made to stand, and women to fall."

SIXTEEN-STRING JACK

The Dandy Highwayman

John Rann, also known as "Sixteen-string Jack", was born in Bath in the 18th century. He worked as a pedlar, a household servant, a stable lad and, lastly, as a coachman, when he became something of a fashion victim. He began wearing the sixteen ribbons tied at his knees for which, as a highwayman, he was to become famous. In September 1774, Rann was arrested for robbery. At his trial he wore a new suit of pea green, a hat with silver strings, a ruffled shirt – and a smile. Though he expected to be acquitted, when the death sentence was passed he remained composed. The night before he died he threw a party for himself and seven girls!

CRIME AND PUNISHMENT

Olde Worlde Justice

In ancient China, the punishment for shoplifting was to brand the offender's forehead with an iron. Thieves had their noses cut off and drunks were strangled.

In Rhode Island, USA, in 1771, William Carlisle was convicted of passing forged dollars. He was sentenced to have both his ears cut off and to be branded on both cheeks with the letter R for "Rogue".

The Ducking Stool was a medieval method of punishment for nags and brawlers, who were sat in a chair fixed to beams and hung over a pond to be plunged into the water as often as their sentence directed.

"Red Letters" were a way of shaming wrongdoers of old. A letter, cut out of cloth, was sewn onto the wrongdoer's clothing. "V" stood for "viciousness", "A" for adultery, "D" for public drunkenness. The victim had to wear the letter for as long as the sentence decreed, sometimes for life. Anyone caught out and about without their letter on could expect to be publicly whipped.

Medieval thieves and drunkards were put in the stocks – a wooden bench with leg-irons – in the village square for people to mock.

Dishonest traders were put in a pillory – a board with holes for the head and hands. Passers-by could throw dung at them.

A "Scold's Bridle" was an iron cage fitted round the head and into the mouth of a nagging wife to keep her quiet. Some had spiked tongue plates for added discomfort.

OLD BILL

Police Facts & Figures

British police have many nicknames, one of which is "Old Bill". According to Scotland Yard, there are several possible reasons why:

Kaiser Wilhelm I of Prussia visited England around the time, in 1864, when the police uniform changed from top hat and swallowtail coat to helmet and tunic. His nickname was Kaiser Bill.

An "old bill" was, in Victorian times, any banknote presumed to be presented to the police for a bribe to persuade them to turn a blind eye to some criminal activity.

New laws for the police to enforce all come from "Bills" passed through Parliament.

Many police officers wore moustaches like that adorning a famous cartoon character, "Old Bill, the wily old soldier in the trenches" created by Bruce Bairnsfather. In 1917, the Government used Bairnsfather's character in posters and advertisements putting over wartime messages under the heading "Old Bill says". For this campaign, the character was dressed in a special constable's uniform.

Old Bill might refer to the Bill Bailey of an old music hall song "Won't You Come Home, Bill Bailey?" The Central Criminal Court is called the Old Bailey.

The London County Council at one time registered all police, fire and ambulance vehicles with the letters BYL.

Robert Peel was behind the law creating the first police force in England. In 1829, his Metropolitan Police Act was passed by the Government. It applied only to London.

London's police were the responsibility of the Home Secretary, with headquarters at Scotland Yard. A thousand men were recruited, and being a policeman became a full-time job with a uniform and weekly pay of 16 shillings.

"Bobbies" or "Peelers" (nicknames that came from Robert Peel) were not popular. Most citizens viewed constables as interfering busybodies, and people often jeered the police. The police were successful though, and crime and disorder declined.

But while central London's crime-rate fell, that of nearby areas increased. Wandsworth became known as "black" Wandsworth because of all the criminals who lived there.

The police in Portland, Oregon, USA, are helped by a pot-bellied pig called Harley, who has been trained to sniff out illegal drugs and guns.

DUMB CRIMINALS

Truly Stupid Criminals

In 1997, a man in North Carolina, USA, broke into a bank's basement through a window, cutting himself in the process. He found that he could neither reach the money from where he was, nor get out of the window through which he had entered. So he thought for a while, then called the police.

In Messina, Italy, Furio Romano snatched a gold chain from around a woman's neck and sprinted away down the street. He stuffed the chain in his mouth as he ran, accidentally sucked the necklace down his windpipe and fell choking to the ground. Luckily for him the cops were close behind and saved his life before arresting him.

A pair of Michigan, USA, robbers entered a record shop nervously waving revolvers. The first one shouted, "Nobody move!" When his partner moved, the first bandit, startled, shot him.

A man walked into a store in Los Angeles, put a 20-dollar bill on the counter and asked for change. When the clerk opened the cash drawer, the man pulled a gun and asked for all the cash, which the clerk promptly gave him. The man took the cash from the clerk and fled, leaving the 20-dollar bill on the counter. The total amount of cash he got from the drawer? Fifteen dollars.

In Oslo, Norway, in 2003, a burglar picked the wrong apartment to rob. The flat was the one used for Norway's version of *Big Brother*. He was filmed by 17 video cameras which recorded his every move and the whole thing was shown live on the internet.

In Nottinghamshire, a girl snatched a woman's purse containing a little cash and a mobile phone. A short time later, the woman's husband decided to call the phone's number. Someone answered the phone but didn't say anything. In the background the husband heard someone order a Big Mac, so he went to the nearest McDonald's and once inside, called again. The phone rang and this time the husband was close enough to see the thief pick it up and answer. She gave up the phone and the purse without a fight.

Shawn West from New Jersey, USA, was trying to rob a sweets and drinks kiosk on the coast. The kiosk was protected by a metal roller door, and Shawn was fashionably dressed in a pair of extremely baggy jeans. When West broke the lock, the door of the stand went up, catching on his jeans. In the morning, the cops found the 17-year-old high up in the air.

In Chicago, USA, Thomas Ingram and two friends broke into a closed restaurant and managed to escape with an automatic cash machine. They squeezed it into the back seat of their car, leaving the back door half open and the machine partially hanging out. Not surprisingly, this attracted a police officer who pulled them over and arrested them. He was able to inform them that the cash machine had been out of order and empty of cash for two years – the restaurant owner had been trying to figure out how to get rid of it.

In Launceston, Australia, a gang tried to rob a cash machine in a shopping centre. They had stolen some welding equipment, which they used to cut open the machine. After several minutes of work, the money in the machine burst into flames and was reduced to ashes.

In 1998, Jason Emmons walked into a corner shop in Tennessee, USA, with a shotgun and demanded all of the money from the till. After the cashier put the money in a bag, the man demanded a bottle of whisky he saw behind the counter. The cashier refused to hand it over because he didn't believe the man was old enough to drink alcohol. Finally, the robber handed over his ID and proved that he was 21. After he left, the cashier called the police and gave them the robber's name and address. Jason was arrested two hours later.

In Indiana, USA, Christopher Adams was pulled over for a minor traffic offence. While talking to him, the officer couldn't help but notice his bright orange T-shirt which read, "Fugitive. You never saw me". He ran Adams' name through the computer and, sure enough, he was indeed a fugitive, wanted for failure to appear at a court hearing. Adams went to jail.

In Mount Shasta, California, Joy Glassman was a loving mother who wanted her sons to get on in life, but she went too far. Her sons grew up to be firemen, and Joy deliberately set fires to help their careers. In 1995, after the fifth one, she was arrested.

In Texas, USA, Andre Meyers held up a convenience store, getting away with some cash and fleeing on foot. He ran to a nearby car park where his getaway car and driver were waiting. They sped away – for about seven metres (20 feet), before they ran out of petrol. They were still trying to re-start the car when the police arrived.

In Mexico City, a man entered a bakery at eight one morning, flashed a knife and demanded a slice of chocolate cake. He enjoyed it so much he was back the next morning for more. And the next day. And the next. On the fifth day the police were waiting for him.

In London, Andrew Collins stole a woman's bank debit card. He headed to the local betting shop where he used the card to place two bets on horse races. Both his horses came in and he won £300. But, since he'd used a debit card and couldn't show proper ID, the betting shop simply paid the winnings into the debit card account rather than paying him in cash as he had expected. The woman whose card was stolen actually ended up £300 better off, and the thief was arrested.

During Prohibition, the consumption of alcohol was banned in the United States. A jury for an illegal alcohol smuggling, or "bootlegging", case in Los Angeles was put on trial after it drank the evidence. The jurors argued that they had sampled the evidence to determine if it contained alcohol, which it did.
However, because they had consumed the evidence, the defendant charged with bootlegging had to be acquitted.

In California, a man robbing a bank demanded that the clerks give him all the money. They asked him to go and sit in his car and they would bring the money out. He agreed. The people in the bank called the police, and when they got there he was still sitting in his car waiting. They arrested him.

In Missouri, USA, Michael Massey was caught trying to steal six 160-kilogram (350-pound) transformers from a local power company. He said he needed them to power a time machine he was building in order to travel into the future and get the lottery numbers.

In ancient Greece, a statue was built of a famous boxer named Theagenes after his death. A jealous rival attacked the statue one night and it fell over and killed him. The dead man's family took the statue to court, where it was found guilty of murder and thrown out of the country.

In Hitachi, Japan, a robber burst into a shop armed with a knife and demanded cash. In the middle of the robbery he realised he'd forgotten to wear his mask. Realising that without it capture was almost certain, he put away his weapon and asked the shopkeeper to please call the police. The shopkeeper did so and the robber explained his predicament to the police, asking them to come over and arrest him as soon as conveniently possible. They were glad to do so.

In Penrith, Australia, a gang smashed their truck through the window of a petrol station. Then they attached a chain to the cash machine inside. They connected the chain to the rear of their truck and sped away. As they dragged the heavy machine through the city streets, sparks flew from under the machine, eventually setting fire to the truck. The gang bailed out before the truck exploded.

A 27-year-old man in New York broke into a house and decided he liked a pair of trousers he found in there better than the ones he was wearing, so he got changed. Police tracked him down after they found his name and address in the pocket of the jeans he had left behind.

In Idaho, USA, a woman's getaway was ruined when she ran out of the shop she had just robbed and jumped into what she thought was a taxi. It was a police car.

In Bucharest, Romania, two burglars put the socks they were wearing on their hands to avoid leaving behind any fingerprints when they robbed a phone shop. The socks smelled so strongly that a police dog was able to track them from the shop all the way to their hiding place, and they were under arrest less than two hours later.

Nolan Preston broke into a hospital in Wiltshire and stole some pagers. Then he spotted a tanning bed. Feeling a little pale, he jumped in and set the timer for 45 minutes. Unfortunately for him, this was not a tanning bed but a special ultra-violet light machine for burn victims and only supposed to be used for ten seconds at a time. Preston was arrested by the police when he arrived to be treated for his injuries at a second hospital, still wearing the doctor's coat he had stolen from the first.

In Bath, England, two thieves snatched the purse of Pamela McCarthy and ran off down the street. What they didn't know was that 40-year-old Pamela was a marathon runner and she chased them for more than a mile before they finally ran into their house. She then called the police who came over and arrested them.

A convicted burglar was being escorted to jail in Florida, USA, when he managed to break loose and flee. During his escape, he suffered a number of cuts on his feet, but was still able to outrun the cops. Police searched the area but the man had completely vanished. However, they got a break in the case when the local hospital called to say that they were treating a man who might be a fugitive. It seems that the escapee had filled out his hospital form giving the "reason or cause of injury" as "escape from jail".

A judge in Kentucky, USA, decided a jury went "a little bit too far" in recommending a sentence of 5,005 years for a man who was convicted of five robberies and a kidnapping. The judge reduced the sentence to 1,001 years.

In Bruno d'Asti, Italy, Carlo Brunelli held up a post office at gunpoint, fleeing with about £2,500. Postal employees locked the door after Brunelli fled and watched as he got into his car, sat there for a moment and then ran back to the door of the post office. Finding it locked, he began to shout for them to please let him in, as he'd left his car keys on the counter. He was still shouting when the police arrived.

Two men tried to pull the front off a cash machine by running a chain from the machine to the bumper of their pick-up truck. Instead of pulling the front panel off the machine, though, they pulled the bumper off their truck. Scared, they left the scene and drove home – leaving the chain still attached to the machine, which was still attached to their bumper and licence plate.

In Bangkok, Thailand, after stealing a woman's purse, a man ran into a building that he thought was a Buddhist temple. He figured that he couldn't be arrested in there. Unfortunately for him, the building was a police station. He was arrested.

In Michigan, USA, the *Ann Arbor News* reported that a man failed to rob a Burger King because the clerk told him he couldn't open the cash register without a food order. So the man ordered onion rings, but the clerk informed him that they weren't available for breakfast, so the robber left.

In Pittsburgh, USA, Robert Nolan held up two convenience stores in one night. He was confronted and arrested by the police outside his own house the following day. How did the police find him so quickly? His getaway van had "Nolan Plumbing and Heating" written on the side in great big letters.

In Missouri, USA, a gunman robbed a 7/11 shop, but returned the money minutes later because his car wouldn't start. Amazingly, the store clerks came out to the car park and gave the robber's car a push. Police officer David Kuppler commented: "We have a very friendly town out here."

A would-be robber had been casing a Boston, USA, bank for several days, waiting for just the right moment to commit a robbery. He queued for the counter, and as he approached the window, he produced a handgun and announced loudly, "THIS IS A HOLD-UP, NOBODY MOVE!" Much to his dismay, the next five customers in line happened to be armed FBI agents on their lunch breaks, waiting to cash their pay cheques. He quickly surrendered with no shots fired. He had failed to notice the FBI Office, which was right next door to the bank.

In Arizona, USA, Michael Jardine tried to rob a shop with a toy gun, which broke when he dropped it on the floor. He ran off, but later tried to rob a supermarket, spraying a shop assistant with pepper spray and trying to grab cash out of her till. She slammed it shut before he could get the cash, and he started having an asthma attack brought on by his own pepper spray. He struggled to his car only to find he had locked the keys inside. He grabbed a rock, smashed his own window and sped away only to be stopped by the police a few minutes later for driving without his headlights on.

A teenager in New Hampshire, USA, robbed a local convenience store of a couple of pocketfuls of change. He walked home. However, he failed to notice the holes in his pockets, and the trail of dropped change led police directly to his house.

In Rangiora, New Zealand, Michael Burns and his two accomplices made careful plans to break into a tobacco shop. First, they cut the wire leading to the burglar alarm, after which they had all the time in the world to help themselves to cash, cigarettes and even to celebrate with a fine cigar. But before the trio could make their getaway, police were on the scene. The burglar alarm they disconnected was for the shop next door. The one in the tobacco shop was still working just fine.

In Virginia, USA, two men in a pick-up truck went to a new-home site to steal a refrigerator. Bumping into walls, they hauled a fridge from one of the houses and loaded it onto the truck. The truck got stuck in the mud, so the robbers decided that the fridge was too heavy. Bumping into the walls again, they put the fridge back. Returning to the truck, they found that they had locked the keys in it. So they left on foot.

Wayne Black, a suspected thief, had his own name tattooed on his forehead. When confronted by police in April 1998, Black insisted he wasn't Wayne Black. To prove it, he stood in front of a mirror and insisted he was Kcalb Enyaw.

An Indiana, USA, a man told a bystander that he was going to rob a convenience store and gave him a dollar, asking him to go into the store to buy a scarf that he would then use to conceal his identity when he carried out the robbery. The bystander went into the store and used the dollar to call the police.

Surprised while burgling a house in Antwerp, Belgium, a thief fled out of the back door, clambered over a three-metre (nine-foot) wall, dropped down and found himself in the city prison.

In Miami, USA, a man walked into a bank, pulled out his gun and demanded money. After the bank teller filled his bag with loot, the man turned to leave and stuffed the gun back into his pocket. The gun fired, shooting him in the leg. He was able to limp out of the bank and shuffled into the street, where he was hit by a van. He was still able to stagger to his getaway car, but not before spitting out two gold teeth that were knocked loose in the accident. Police tracked him down through his dental records.

Two young car thieves in Florida, USA, appeared before the judge after stealing their 25th car in just two years. After the boys were released, they walked out of the court and discovered they did not have bus fare for a ride home. So the duo stole car number 26, which they crashed into a fence.

In 2003, a man in Zwickau, Germany, broke into a butcher's shop with his dog, Lumpi. He set off an alarm and attempted to run, but Lumpi was still eating sausages when the police arrived and both were apprehended.

In Canberra, Australia, Norman Parker went shopping at a department store and found a sweater he liked. He took it into one of the changing rooms, removed the security tag, stuffed the sweater underneath his jacket and headed for the door. However, the security alarm went off just as he was passing through. How could this have happened? Because when he had removed the security tag, he had put it in his pocket.

In California, USA, a burglar decided that he just couldn't leave without taking a bath in a large bathtub he found. He was still there when the police arrived.

CRIME FILES

Various Criminal Activities

In 2002, a police camera in Gluckstedt, Germany, snapped a duck breaking the speed limit – 39 km/h (24 mph) in a 30 zone.

In Britain, anyone can make a "citizen's arrest". But while the police can arrest a person on suspicion of an offence, other people can only arrest someone they have actually seen committing a crime. Resisting arrest is a crime whether the arrest is made by police or others.

The word "testify" comes from the custom of men in ancient Roman courts swearing to a statement by placing their hand over their testicles.

It was common in the 1930s for gangsters to carry guns wrapped in newspapers. Due to the large size of certain US newspapers in the 1920s and the early part of the 1930s (papers were almost twice the size they are today), even a machine gun could be concealed. Bullets could be fired from guns inside rolled-up newspapers much more efficiently than from a violin case, which is the more usual hiding place in gangster movies.

United States President Franklin Pierce was arrested while in office for running over an old woman with his horse, but the case was dropped due to insufficient evidence in 1853.

The Bible is not only the best-selling book of all time, it is also the book most often stolen from bookshops in the USA.

In England, murder is murder. There are no degrees of murder, as in the United States.

A number of religious groups – for example the Jehovah's Witnesses and the Plymouth Brethren – are not permitted to judge other people's actions, and therefore say that they would be unable to take part in jury decision-making. Excusal on this basis has been permitted by law in the UK only in the last few years – before that, the issue had to be argued every time a juror was summoned.

The Beefeaters who guard the Tower of London are properly called Yeoman Warders. A perk of the job originally was a daily allowance of beer and beef, an expensive luxury out of reach of the ordinary working citizen. "Beefeaters" was a nickname awarded the Warders out of jealousy for their cushy position.

In Kirkland, Illinois, USA, it is illegal for bees to fly over the village or through any of its streets.

The first recorded incident of a drunk-driving conviction was in 2800 BC. In ancient Egypt, an inebriated charioteer was apprehended after running down a vestal virgin of the goddess Hathor. The culprit was crucified on the door of the tavern that sold him the beer, and his corpse allowed to hang there until scavengers had reduced it to bones.

The town council of Gold Hill, Oregon, USA, voted to fire Police Chief Katie Holmboe for selling Mary Kay cosmetics out of her police car and praying on behalf of a suspect she believed was possessed by the devil.

A man in Colorado, USA, was arrested for roller-skating down a steep section of road. He was charged with speeding and running a stop sign. The speed limit was 72 km/h (45 mph).

The expression "daylight robbery" came from highwaymen who held up travellers in broad daylight rather than at night – a very brazen act which was obvious to anyone looking on and made identification of the highwayman easier. It therefore came to mean a blatant and obvious act of theft.

New York was the first American state to require the licensing of motor vehicles. The law was adopted in 1901.

The vast majority of police cars in Britain are white, but in London, red police cars are driven by officers of the Royalty and Diplomatic Protection Group. In addition to close protection of members of the Royal Family, the group is also responsible for the security of foreign embassies and the protection of politicians and diplomats from home or abroad.

In the USA, federal law states that children's TV shows may contain only ten minutes of advertising per hour and on weekends the limit is ten and a half minutes.

Oxford University requires all members upon admission to the Bodleian Library to read aloud a pledge that includes an agreement to not "kindle therein any fire or flame". Regulations also prohibit readers bringing sheep into the library.

Over 16,000 Americans have received new identities under the Federal Witness Security Program.

Bowling used to be done with nine pins. When a law was passed in colonial Connecticut making "bowling at nine pins" illegal, those who ran the games simply started using ten pins.

Temperature and crime are correlated. Many more crimes are committed in the hot summer months than in the cold winter months.

In 1658, Paris police raided a monastery and sent twelve monks to jail for eating meat and drinking wine during Lent.

A stolen car is 200 times more likely to get into a crash than other cars.

Jack the Ripper, the notorious murderer in 19th-century England, committed his crimes only at weekends.

Organised crime is estimated to account for 10% of the United States' entire annual national income.

Half of all crimes in the USA are committed by people under the age of 18, and 80% of burglaries are committed by people aged 13–21.

In Bangkok, Thailand, in 1996, police searched the men's toilets of Thailand's Parliament after an anonymous bomb threat was phoned in. They got a surprise. They found a box they feared contained a bomb, but discovered instead that it contained a monitor lizard. The *Bangkok Post* headline the following day was: "Lizard fails to explode in MPs' toilet".

In the USA, the Eisenhower Interstate System requires that one mile in every five must be straight. These straight sections are usable as airstrips in times of war or other emergencies.

Licenced London taxis (black cabs) are required by law to carry a bale of hay at all times. This dates from the days of the horse-drawn cab, and the law has never been revoked.

A monkey was once tried and convicted for smoking a cigarette in South Bend, Indiana, USA.

In Britain, the law was changed in 1789 to make hanging the method of execution. Prior to that, burning was the usual sentence.

The greatest funeral for a Chicago gangster ever held was for a flower shop entrepreneur named Dion O'Banion. The shop, at the corner of State and Superior Streets, was a front for O'Banion's bootlegging and hijacking operations. Ten thousand mourners were in attendance, and the most expensive wreath – it cost $1,000 – came from Al Capone, who had ordered that O'Banion be killed.

In 1979, 14 children aged ten years old or younger were charged with murder in the United States.

BBC TV's *Crimewatch* **programme shows reconstructions of real crimes to help the police catch real criminals. Soon after watching one** *Crimewatch* **reconstruction, a police officer on duty noticed a man with similar looks and build to the criminal, and attempted to arrest him. He discovered that the man in question was the actor** *Crimewatch* **had employed in the reconstruction.**

In 1861, John Wentworth fired the entire Chicago Police Department when his term as mayor came to an end. He fired sixty patrolmen, three sergeants, three lieutenants, and one captain. The city was entirely without police protection for twelve hours until the Board of Commissioners swore in new officers.

The murder of a brother is called "fratricide" and murder of a sister, "sororicide".

In 17th-century Japan, no citizen was allowed to leave the country on penalty of death. Anyone caught coming in or going out without permission was executed on the spot.

In Tsu, Japan, a robber marched into a bank and demanded cash. Employees led him to the bank's main vault but when he went inside to grab his cash, they closed the door, locking him inside. And that's where he stayed until the police turned up.

The Tower of London – for which construction was begun in 1078 by William the Conqueror – is currently the home of the British Crown Jewels and is a major tourist attraction. In its time, it has also housed a prison and place of execution, and served as an observatory, a mint, a zoo and a royal palace.

During the time that the atomic bomb was being developed by the United States at Los Alamos, New Mexico, security in the building was very strict and military secrets were under tight protection. So much so that applicants for routine jobs, like cleaners and decorators, were disqualified if they could read. Illiteracy was a legal job requirement.

In Japan, where kissing was considered (by Tokyo's Prefect of Police) to be "unclean, immodest, indecorous, ungraceful, and likely to spread disease", about 240 kilometres (150 miles) of kissing scenes were deleted from US movies released there in 1926.

In most American states, a wedding ring is exempt by law from inclusion among the assets in a bankruptcy estate. This means that a wedding ring cannot be seized by creditors, no matter how much the bankrupt person owes.

In 1967, the CIA fitted a known criminal's pet cat with high-tech listening equipment. Ten minutes after the cat was released, it was run over by a taxi.

In 1671, the notorious spy and wanted outlaw Thomas Blood attempted to steal the Crown Jewels from the Tower of London. He and his gang were captured and imprisoned in the Tower. Blood refused to speak to anyone except King Charles himself, who agreed to see him at Whitehall. On July 18th, 1671, instead of being hanged for treason, Blood was released from his prison cell, had his properties restored to him and was granted a pension of £500 per year by the King. Why King Charles released him remains a mystery to this day.

The country of Togo has the lowest crime rate in the world, with an average of just 11 reported crimes annually for every 100,000 of the population.

BEHIND BARS

Prisoners' Tales

In Belo Horizonte, Brazil, a prisoner escaped on foot from the police jail. He had not gone very far when he saw a bus approaching. He hailed the bus and got on, where he discovered that inside the bus were ten city policemen on their way to look for him. He returned to jail.

Nearly 43% of convicted criminals serving prison sentences in the USA are re-arrested within a year of being released from prison.

There are more people in prison in the United States than there are people living in Tuscon, Arizona.

In the 102 prisons in the USA, 93% of inmates are men. The average age of an inmate is 37, and the most common sentence is 5–10 years.

In Alberta, Canada, prisoner Raymond Tyree tried to pull a daring escape. He crawled into the prison's ventilation system, intending to make his way to an outside wall. Round and round he crawled, avoiding capture but never finding a way out. Other prisoners took pity on him and left him food and water. Eventually, prison officials tracked him down, two months later and 13 kilograms (30 pounds) lighter.

Marie-Augustin Marquis de Pelier was arrested in 1786 and spent the next 50 years in prison. His crime? Whistling at Queen Marie Antoinette as she was being ushered into a theatre.

The slogan on New Hampshire car licence plates in the US is "Live Free or Die". These licence plates are manufactured by prisoners in the state prison in Concord.

Herman Melville, the author of whale story *Moby Dick*, was once imprisoned in Tahiti as a mutineer, but he was able to escape.

In Zephyrhills, Florida, USA, prisoner Korey Hardy stole his orange prison uniform when he was released. He then wore it to a rock concert, where he drew the attention of one of the 200 police officers working as security at the venue. He was escorted back to jail.

Ironically, the maximum security prison in Saint Albans, Vermont, USA, was responsible in 1996 for sending out holiday brochures enticing tourists to visit Vermont.

Yugoslavian prisoner Savo Radovanovic had been waiting for quite some time to be transferred from one jail to another. Thinking things had to be better in the new place, and getting tired of the wait, he decided to take matters into his own hands. He broke out of jail and while police were conducting a nationwide manhunt for him, he turned up at the front gates of the other prison and was apprehended while trying to break in.

The famed Alcatraz prison in San Francisco Bay was first used as a prison by the army during the US Civil War. Numerous escapes were attempted; however, there is no firm evidence that any succeeded. The word "alcatraz" is Spanish for "pelican".

There have been about 30 films made at or about Alcatraz, including *The Rock* (1996), *Birdman of Alcatraz* (1962), and *Escape from Alcatraz* (1979).

Alcatraz inmates have included gangsters Al Capone, Machine-gun Kelly and Floyd Hamilton, the getaway driver for notorious bank robbers Bonny and Clyde.

Queen Elizabeth I of England scratched the following message on her prison window using a diamond:
"Much suspected of me,
Nothing proved can be."

Each week in the United States, the population of state and federal prison increases by about 1,000.

One out of every 43 American prisoners escapes from prison. 94% are recaptured.

North Dakota and New Hampshire have fewer people in jail per head of population than any other American state.

IT'S A DIFFERENT LANGUAGE

Criminal Phrases & Codes

Police in the US use ten codes to let each other know what's going on. You may have heard "10-4" meaning "OK", but here are a few others:

10-0	use caution
10-1	cannot receive you
10-2	receive you OK
10-3	stop transmitting
10-4	OK, I acknowledge
10-5	pass on this message
10-7	out of service
10-8	available for incidents
10-9	repeat your transmission
10-10	off duty
10-12	stand by

10-31	crime in progress
10-32	subject with gun
10-33	alarm sounding, emergency
10-34	a riot
10-37	suspicious vehicle
10-39	urgent – use lights and siren
10-40	silent response
10-41	beginning tour of duty
10-42	ending tour of duty
10-49	broken traffic light
10-50	accident
10-52	ambulance needed
10-54	animals on highway
10-67	person calling for help
10-70	fire alarm
10-74	negative
10-77	estimated time of arrival
10-78	need assistance
10-86	officer on duty
10-90	bank alarm
10-98	jail break
11-99	officer needs help

A criminal organisation will sometimes hire gunmen. These are called "goons", "hatchetmen", "torpedoes", or "trigger men".

Opening a safe is a special job among criminals. A "can opener" or "yegg" can open cheap safes, but a "Peterman" uses nitroglycerine, or "soup" to blow the safe.

To Chicago gangsters, a gun could be a "bean-shooter", "gat", "rod" or "roscoe".

Jack Ketch was a well known hangman in old England. When a pirate "Danced with Jack Ketch", he went to the gallows. And "Pieces of Eight"? These were Spanish silver coins worth one peso or eight reales. There were sometimes literally cut into eight pieces, each piece worth one real.

A "Chicago overcoat" was gangster slang for a coffin.

"BOLO" is short for "Be On the Look Out", a police alert to watch out for something or someone.

Police investigators are experts in collecting "dactylograms", otherwise known as fingerprints.

The Omertà is the Mafia code of silence and one of the premier vows taken when being sworn into the "Family". Violation of the code is punishable by death.

The "Jaws of Life" is a heavy rescue tool used by police and emergency services to pry open vehicles. It is similar in shape to a pair of pliers, only much larger and driven by hydraulics or air pressure. It is fully capable of cutting a car in half.

When New York policemen have a party, they call it "Choir Practice".

A "duffer" is Australian slang for a
cattle thief.

**The Police Radio Alphabet allows cops to
spell words, names and addresses so that
there is no confusion. So "Hotel Echo Lima
Papa" would spell out "Help!"**

ALPHA	**A**	**N**	NOVEMBER
BRAVO	**B**	**O**	OSCAR
CHARLIE	**C**	**P**	PAPA
DELTA	**D**	**Q**	QUEBEC
ECHO	**E**	**R**	ROMEO
FOXTROT	**F**	**S**	SIERRA
GOLF	**G**	**T**	TANGO
HOTEL	**H**	**U**	UNIFORM
INDIA	**I**	**V**	VICTOR
JULIET	**J**	**W**	WHISKY
KILO	**K**	**X**	X-RAY
LIMA	**L**	**Y**	YANKEE
MIKE	**M**	**Z**	ZULU

A STICKY END

Criminals' Undesirable Executions

In 1844, Jonathan Walker was the last person branded in the US as punishment for a crime. He had the initials "SS" branded into the palm of his right hand as punishment for helping American slaves escape to the Bahamas. (The charge against him was "slave stealing".)

The last public execution in America was the hanging of 22-year-old Rainey Bethea at Owensboro, Kentucky in 1936. He had been convicted of murdering a 70-year-old woman. 20,000 people including over 200 sheriffs and deputies from various parts of the USA gathered to watch.

Strange as it may seem, Doctor Joseph Ignace Guillotin wanted to get rid of the death penalty in 18th-century France. Some executions at the time were by "quartering", where a prisoner's limbs were tied to four oxen and the animals driven in different directions, tearing the victim apart. Guillotin wanted a painless capital punishment method, as a step towards banning the death penalty altogether, so he came up with the guillotine, a machine for chopping off heads. Its first use was on April 25, 1792, when highwayman Nicolas Jacques Pelletier lost his head at Place de Grève in Paris. Thousands of aristocrats, including the king, were guillotined during the French Revolution, and the last guillotining took place in Marseilles on September 10, 1977, when the murderer, Hamida Djandoubi, was beheaded.

The last woman to be executed by burning in England was Christian Bowman in 1789. Her crime was making counterfeit coins.

Sir William Wallace, the Scottish rebel portrayed in the film *Braveheart*, **was "hanged, drawn and quartered", a horrible execution which involved chopping a person into pieces, preferably while still alive. His head was placed on a pole on London Bridge, his right arm was hung above a bridge in Newcastle, his left arm was sent to Berwick, his right foot and leg to Perth and his left quarter to Aberdeen where it was buried in what is now the wall at St Machar's Cathedral.**

In 1941, Josef Jakobs, a German spy, became the last person to be executed in the Tower of London, England.

Sheep theft is still legally a hangable offence in Scotland.

In France in 1740, a cow was found guilty of sorcery and was hanged.

If you enjoyed this book, you can find more amazing facts in the following books:

Title	ISBN
1000 of the World's Most Astonishing Facts	0 603 56067 9
The World's Most Amazing Animal Facts for Kids	0 603 56060 1
The World's Most Amazing Battle Facts for Kids	0 603 56098 9
The World's Most Amazing Inventions Facts for Kids	0 603 56099 7
The World's Most Amazing Monster Facts for Kids	0 603 56104 7
The World's Most Amazing Planet Earth Facts for Kids	0 603 56062 8
The World's Most Amazing Science Facts for Kids	0 603 56062 8